Blind Spots

Bruce Dawe

Blind Spots

A verse play

PICARO PRESS

Blind Spots: A verse play
ISBN 978 1 921691 68 3
Copyright © text Bruce Dawe 2013

First published by Picaro Press 2013

This edition published 2015 by
Picaro Press – an imprint of
GINNINDERRA PRESS
PO Box 3461 Port Adelaide 5015 Australia
www.ginninderrapress.com.au

for Barney Cooney
for his many years of friendship

Cast of Characters

Ozzie Manning

Woman

Man

Kevin Rudd

Julia Gillard

Faceless Men

Media Representatives

Pork Barrellers

Cartoonist

Tony Abbott

Mark Latham

Swinging Voter

Indies

Coalition Senator

Miners

News Media Announcer

Dr Bob Brown

Professor Dudley

Peter Garrett

Illegal Immigrants

Dancing Girls

Act One

[OZZIE MANNING, A middle-aged male, sits facing the audience, in a lounge chair. Newspapers are draped over an arm of his chair. A TV set is angled away from the audience. He has a bottle of beer on a side-table and his feet are up on a stool.]

OZZIE: My name is Ozzie Manning
When I'm sittin' here at home
(Which is most of the time, as anyone can see…).
I'm that so-called Average Aussie
But I'm not so keen to roam:
A 'couch-potato's' what I generally choose to be…

I don't get paid for sittin' here,
Not like those other blokes
On the radio, in the papers, and on telly,
But I've still got views about 'em:
A lot of 'em are jokes,
Like *feet*: some sweet, some sour, some even smelly!

[MAN and WOMAN enter. Their speeches express the initial excitement of Rudd's election as PM]

WOMAN: Let's start the show with someone you know
(Or *thought* you did, to begin with!):
He seemed the sort of jack-in-the-box
Any party looked certain to win with…

And *win* they did! And he seemed at first
A leader sent from heaven…
Yes, you've guessed it already, folks!
That maestro's name was…KEVIN!

[Crowd noises, 'We want Kevin', etc.]

MAN: And so, when Kevin 07 rode out of the North
We waited to hear just what words would pour forth:
There were BIG WORDS a-plenty (we were very impressed)
We could understand *some* and mumbled the rest,

WOMAN: And on Sundays we saw him, Thérèse by his side,
Bothering God too (who for certain replied)
And soon we were comforted to hear and to see
Kevin quoting Bonhoeffer for *his* the-ol-ogy,
That brave German martyr thus leading the way
For Kevin to follow at a much later day.

MAN: Well, we'd had PMs before who kept some people busy,
But Kevin 07 had us *all* in a tizzy
– The paperwork flowed from his pro-active brain
And we wondered: How long can he stand the great strain?
To Washington he went then to greet the Obamas…

WOMAN: But he'd hardly had time to get out of his pyjamas
Before he was off to shake hands with some men
Who might find him a Council seat at the UN…

TOGETHER: The media loved him, his poll ratings soared
To 70% – what a wizard, good Lord!

[Exit WOMAN and MAN.]

OZZIE: Kev's plans were big and BIGGER
And the surplus in Oz was a figure
Big enough (Wayne said) to beat that GFC…
So, being super-high-octane-powered,
Thanks to a Scrooge called Howard,
Kev spent up like a drunken sailor out on a spree!

[Lights flicker, dim.]

But…one night when the lights were low,
Someone let those pink batts go,
And those warm and fuzzy feelin's started to dim…
Poor Peter was sent to the garret,
The *stick* replaced the *carrot*
And that was the last the public heard from *him!*

[Enter KEVIN bemused, groping around, eventually finds chair, sits down.]

KEVIN: Though the heavens above are clear
It's not the same down here.
What happened (I keep asking myself)
On the way from the Forum?
In a couple of years or so
I went from Go! to Woe
When I lost my crown but not (thank God!) my decorum…

Once I sat there in pride of place
A bright look all over my face
I had the best chair there is in Parliament House.
Now here, on the backest bench,
It's quite an imaginative wrench
When you move from being top-dog to a top dog's louse!

Old Mao Zedong would know,
He ran a similar show;
His gang of four was really a Gang of *One*…
Ah well, *he* lies in state…
It's tough to be stuffed, old mate,
But at least *his* image still shines there in the sun!

[KEVIN sings to the tune of 'My Bonny Lies Over the Ocean!']

Oh once I had a great caucus,
As submissive as ever could be,
It left all the important decisions
To Julia, Wayne, Lindsay, and me…

It never asked any rude questions
On NBN or EMT,
'Cos Kevin 07 had the answers,
And his wrath was frightening to see!

Chorus:

Bring back, oh bring back,
Oh bring back that caucus to me, to me,
Bring back, oh bring back,
Oh bring back that caucus to me, to me,

And once, too, I had me a cabinet
As polished as any could be,
Oh how I miss it, not havin' it,
Whatever I said, they'd agree.

Oh bring back that caucus so friendly
And that cabinet so close to me
– How was I to see the unseeable,
That they'd indulge in such bleak treachery?

[Chorus repeated.]

Yes, there were Wayne, Lindsay, – and Julia,
For breakfast, luncheon, and tea
– But what I now find quite peculiar
Is what they have *all* done to me.

But now that *they've* brought in the chain-saw,
And I've fallen right out of my tree,
I long for that feather-bed caucus
To provide a soft-landing for me,

[Chorus repeated. Exit KEVIN.]

OZZIE: Well, media folk just *love* labels
To them we're all Daves or Mabels,
And they've got one ready to stick again
On those backroom blokes they call…The Faceless Men!

[Enter two FACELESS MEN, masked, wearing business suits.]

FACELESS MEN (Together): You've heard a lot about us.
And most of it's untrue,
That we're Labour's *Mafiosi*,
And it's sneaky things we do…

[Pretend to stalk around.]

We talk with lots of innocent little
Pollies that we meet,
Behind closed doors, in clubs and pubs,
And in the darkened street,

We tell them what to do and say
We tell them who they must
Give concrete shoes at midnight,
And who is worth their trust…

Don't fall for nasty rumours
Made up by wicked liars
Who back in earlier days we'd burn
Slowly on big fires.

FIRST FACELESS MAN: I'm Bruno and I'm simply here
To help you get things right,
This mask isn't sinister at all;
It's to keep me warm at night.

I'm a backroom boy, it's true, but that's
Because I'm kinda shy.
As a little kid I could never ever dare look
Anyone in the eye…

SECOND FACELESS MAN: *Arrivederci, ciao, bon giorno!*
My famed linguistic skill
Enables me, like Bruno here,
To go in for the kill.

The ones up front, those pollies,
They need our love and care,
Especially since the likes of us
In the *unions* put them there.

They're all of 'em *ravioli*,
Mere *pasta* in our hands,
And we're the top chefs *kneading* them
– In some more distant lands

Like Sicily or Napoli
We'd get paid full respect
– But even here we shape 'em up
And you folks, then, elect…

TOGETHER: Young Kevin, you know, he had to go
(Our Victorian friends agreed),
Though it's never ever nice to see
A fellow *padrone* bleed…

But Julia, now, we feel can give
Our party a new life;
We pray the time will never come
When we have to use the knife…

[Bell begins tolling.]

OZZIE: Y'know, hearin' those latest opinions polls
It's like hearin' the bells for a funeral toll
Which means it's not lookin' good for some poor pollie…
Like when you're in hospital sick
And the doc comes round to tick
Your medical chart with the nurse
And they both look melancholy.

Your temperature's 103
And you're thinkin': That's *it* for me…
And the doctor and nurse just look at each other and nod…
So what can you do or say
Except lie there and quietly pray
And try to think of somethin' you've done
That was pleasin' to GOD?

[KEVIN enters, bedraggled, speaks in a tragic tone.]

KEVIN: All withered now, are the garments that I wore…
My opinion polls have fallen; now, no more
Do my young advisers seem so brightly wise
As when, behind closed doors, they did advise.

The betting's turned against me – I'm odds-on
To get the chopper now my luck has gone,
And anytime, by day or visiting moon,
They'll come for me. I hope they make it soon…

[KEVIN exits. Pause. Off-stage sound of 'Aargh!' as knife goes in.]

Act Two

OZZIE: Mind you, when they'd done the deed,
Kevin wasn't left on the rug to bleed
While the ones who'd done it went right on with their talkin',
No, with a good friend by his side,
He left the meetin' with a steady stride
(Even though, of course, we knew he was a dead man walkin'!...)

[Wedding march begins as JULIA enters, with crown in hand.]

JULIA: The bells are still ringing,
(At least in my ears,)
Some people are cheering,
Others, in tears…

This crown that I'm holding's
Still hard to keep on;
I'm remembering Kevin
And a kingship that's gone.

Oh, I know some are whispering,
And fix me with glares:
'She's got there so quickly!
Do you think she still *cares?*'

Well, let me just tell you,
Right here from the start
– It's not all my doing,
Even though I was part

Of what quite a few people
Elsewhere decided…
Oh, yes, and my *innocence*
Has been often derided!

But I stand here before you
As reluctant a queen
As young Bessie Tudor
Could ever have been…

So why did I nod
And say 'Yes' to this crown?
It was *that*, or my Party
Was doomed to go down.

Or course, there were times
When Kevin was wrong,
And *I* was a theme
In that discordant song.

But *all* voices were lost
In that one-man parade
As people stopped listening
To the marches *he* played.

He was all things to all people…
Or at least, so he thought,
But the sum of his talents
Had shrunken to nought.

'Emergency surgery
Is called for,' they said.
But what surgeon wouldn't mourn for
The patient that's dead?

I'm the first woman PM
To be queen of this land…
That *that* troubled many
I could well understand.

And that ringing in my ears
Could be happening because
I'd cracked *that* glass ceiling
For the first time in Oz.

Please try to think of me
When my time should end,
As you would of a well-meaning,
Now absent, *friend*.

[Lights down. JULIA exits.]

[Media hubbub, background of voices asking questions, competing with each other, etc.]

OZZIE: Well, they talk about our media
As if nothin' could be seedier,
But at least they fill us in on a lot of the action:
Who's presently gettin' up *who*,
Who's foot's in the doggy-do,
And who's centre-half-back (or lock) for a certain *faction*...

[Three MEDIA REPS enter.]

TOGETHER: We're the media, we're the possums
Who present the latest news,
We do what barbers used to do:
We shape your heads – and *views*.

We chatter away to each other, and
To pollies, whenever we can
– Megabytes of this and that,
Since your attention-span

In these days of digital *extractus*
Are very *brief* as we know,
And our *modus operandi*
Is to ensure we keep it so...

MEDIA 1:   We blow on dying embers,

MEDIA 2:   And dying *members* too,

MEDIA 3:   Our major rôle and business
Is to stir up *them* and *you*.

TOGETHER: Through intravenous dripping
We sustain your latent fears,
Bad news our best prescription
– It's worked well for many years.

MEDIA 1:   Do migrants make you nervous?

MEDIA 2:   Do boat-people make you quake?

MEDIA 3:   Is the environment in crisis?

TOGETHER: We will help you lie awake!

MEDIA 1:   Is it flip-flops by the government
Or crime-waves haunt your night?

MEDIA 2:   If you're insecure and fearful,
Then we know we're doing right.

MEDIA 1   And when it comes to PMs…:
We've seen them come and go
(Like good old Robert Menzies
– Before *your* time, we know!).

    Bob Hawke? Well, he was just like one of us,
And swore in public, too,
In such a way you wished the one
He swore at could be *you!*

[MEDIA 2 shakes head sadly.]

But Julia had us baffled:
Julia was unique:
We just couldn't fit her into
Any *pattern* (so to speak…).

She wasn't anybody's Mum,
Nobody praised her cooking,
And yet some people found her
(From *some* angles) quite good-looking.

And, when she felt at ease, she could
(We all agreed) be gracious
– Her smile, then could even make
This up-tight world seem…*spacious*.

MEDIA 3: With that red hair she still could be
A modern Boadicea,
So it might seem a safer bet
To depict her with a sneer…

MEDIA 1: Of course, you wouldn't have spent much time
On what a PM (male)
Wore or how he cut *his* hair,
Or if he had a prominent *tail*,

Or how he *walked*… But, when we were faced
With an unmarried fem,
Who'd become by some mismanagement
Our very own *PM*,

What *else* would serve us half as well,
And discourage any others,
Even if they were *married* with *kids*
And proved to be *model* mothers?!

TOGETHER: Negative campaigning
Is how governments now should go,
Platitudes are safest,
Brands and images all we know.

MEDIA 1: Remember though we'd rather be
Impartial, fair, and just,
It's the advertisers pay the bills,
So dance for *them* we must!

But just in case you're thinking
That all we pitch is poo,
You have to admit in honesty
We do lots of good stuff too!

[Exit MEDIA REPS. Lights up on OZZIE.]

OZZIE: Of course, for a bloke like me
Plonked here in front of TV
I don't get far into the mornin' paper before I'm noddin'.
So I turn to the cartoons first;
They sum everythin' up in one burst
But readin' the rest of the stuff soon has me ploddin'…

[Enter CARTOONIST with easel.]

CARTOONIST: Dear Lord above, we humbly pray
That you will send to us, day after day,
Public figures who can meet
The need for laughter in the street.

On bus, and tram, and crowded train,
We try to make folks laugh again
And, through our cartoon universe,
Feel better, rather than much worse…

> Give us, dear Lord, a bloke who's fat
> (Once, Russell Hinze provided that),
> Or a feature that makes us all feel good
> Like Johnny Howard's eyebrows could,
>
> Or Tony Abbott's ears and those
> Bright budgie-smugglers – and who knows
> But when the Libs voted Malcolm out
> It was Tony's beach-wear had the clout?!
>
> But what cartoonists *love* the most
> Is when some pollie's face plays host
> To one outstanding point that glows
> Like a neon sign, such as…a NOSE!

[Uncovers on easel, large cartoon of JULIA's nose. Kneels addressing the cartoon.]

> Ah, Julia, how deeply in your debt
> We are, because your schnozzer met
> Our deepest needs and our love grows
> And blossoms like your splendid nose!
>
> Lead on, sweet nose, in your new quest,
> May you smell out the least unrest,
> And, unlike Kevin, talk it through
> Lest Kevin's fate should happen to you…

[Exit CARTOOONIST with easel.]

[Enter from right stage three PORK-BARRELLERS. They sing together, to the tune of 'Roll Out the Barrel'. They roll three barrels around. They stop for each of them to sing a verse but join in opening and closing verses. While each one is singing, the others distribute largesse from their barrels.]

TOGETHER: Roll out the barrel,
Pork-barrelling, we mean.
It's a familiar Christmas carol
In the present political scene!

Zing, boom, tarrarel,
The other buggers are on the run!
When it's time to roll out the pork-barrel
Big spending's lots of fun!

PB 1: Government, they tell us,
Is for *all* of us here in Oz
– But the Opposition knows for funding,
They're the has-beens, the old never-was!

PB 2: Y'know, every government wonders
When there's money, how it should be spent:
But with an election coming on
You'll *wonder* where all of it went!

PB 3: Roll out the pork-barrel
(We now call it 'sandbagging', too,
Because money, like sandbags protects us
So the other lot can never flood through…).

We're hearing all of this talk now
Of national networks of fibre
Which means you folks in the cities
Are going to get it up the Khyber!

TOGETHER: Come dressed in your poshest apparel,
Shout all of your voters free beer…
The best time to roll the pork-barrel
Is an election YEAR!

[Exit PORK BARRELLERS with barrels. Lights down briefly. Up on OZZIE.]

OZZIE: Julia went on kissin' babies
And wore a hard-hat, too,
And visited lots of class-rooms
As pollies have to do
Since meet-the-people visitin'
Is a thing they've *got* to LIKE
– Tony was more of an outdoor-boy
At the beach or on his bike…

[TONY enters with an exercise bike.]

TONY: Yes, you can all have a go at me,
I'm no media tart,
But put me on my bicycle
And I'm a work of art!

[TONY gets on exercise bike, pedals along genially during his speech.]

My pedalling keeps me trim and slim,
And registers the fact
Like that Russian fella, Putin,
I'm stripped and ready to *act!*

While others (you know who I mean)
Will mind their Ps and Qs,
And pinch a quote from Hillary
Or Barack – I refuse

To play those kind of nursery games
– I'm Tony, *get the habit!*
Don't take any heed of those
Who call me 'Mr Rabbit'.

I'm the Action-Man campaigner,
What you see, is what you get
– Got a wife and kids, not a partner,
So we're an odds-on bet.

> I've seen 'em come, I've seen 'em go;
> Brendan, and Malcolm too,
> And Peter, he could've had the job
> But he couldn't follow through.
>
> I'd better keep a sharp eye out
> For 'black holes' in the road
> Another billion-dollar hole
> Could see me…well…*implode*!
>
> Meanwhile, like Hubert Opperman,
> I'll pedal this tricky track,
> So, don't be surprised, if I get *pipped*,
> To see me pedalling *back!*

[Lights down on TONY as he exits. Lights up on OZZIE again.]

OZZIE: But of course there's always casualties
    From earlier pollie wars
    And among the *walking wounded,* Mark
    Was keen on settling scores!

[Enter MARK LATHAM. He comes bursting on with mike about to confront a pollie but stops, startled, with none on stage.]

MARK: I'm the spanner in the works,
    I'm the cockroach in the pie,
    I'm the Prince of all the Berks,
    I'm the insect in your eye.

    I'm the bloke that muscles in,
    I'm the man the media *love*,
    With a voice that's nails-on-tin
    (Angels shudder up above).

I'm an 'ex' who never ever
Forgave the world that let me down,
I've moved on from rude and clever
To be Krustier than any Klown.

I'm what happens when the bucket
You've carefully placed above the door
Falls on you and you yell out 'Fuck it!'
As you lie there on the floor.

Yeah, I'm the light bulb that's been blown,
I'm a bloody sun that briefly shone,
I'm the block of rubbled stone
When the shaping sculptor's gone…

[MARK LATHAM wanders off… OZZIE grins, shrugs to the audience.]

OZZIE: At times there's lots of chatter
About one special person
More talked about than Lady Gaga
(Or even Elle McPherson)
A bloke whose votes in the ballot-box
Cause lots of blessin' and cursin'…
But for all the worries *that* bloke gives us
Does he care one iota?
Not on your Nelly! He's the one
They call 'The Swingin' Voter!'

[Enter SWINGING VOTER with low trapeze. He jumps on trapeze, faces audience.]

SWINGING VOTER: Look, I'm the swinging voter
Up here on my trapeze.
You turn to me at election-time
Upon your bended knees!

Sometimes I'm simply swinging
Because I'm quite uncertain
Which candidate deserves my vote
When my hip-pocket's hurtin'.

But perhaps I wouldn't vote at all
In a voluntary system, say,
Like they have in that great democracy
They call the USA,

Or if, as young cynics used to say,
Before they took to sin:
'Whoever it is you vote for,
A *politician* still gets *in!*'

Now candidates in elections know
That 25 per cent
Of voters are up there swinging
And to get them in *your* tent
Is where the game gets tricky
– Like when you're at the zoo,
Luring monkeys with bananas
Is what you've got to do…

But we swingers, just like monkeys,
Have played this game before,
And we often swing more temptingly
The more visiting folk implore.

But, with all these Indie pollies
Swingin' up there in the breeze,
It's getting' kind of crowded
Up here on this trapeze!

[SWINGING VOTER shakes head, moves off stage right with trapeze.]

Act Three

OZZIE: As a special treat this time around,
　　　　So close was *this* election,
　　　　We've got four blokes all keen to spruik
　　　　Our country's *new* direction.

　　　　They're independent MPs who
　　　　For once have got your attention
　　　　With lots of issues to discuss
　　　　(And some they forgot to mention.)

[The INDIES enter dancing, all clutching papers. Each then steps forward and speaks in turn.]

OAKESHOTT: We're the Indies, we're the Indies,
　　　　　　We're the ones from Outer Space,
　　　　　　Nobody ever cared before
　　　　　　If we were in the race.

WINDSOR: We were kinda like Camilla
　　　　　Parker-Bowles was to her Charlie:
　　　　　Only pillion passengers
　　　　　On the REALLY BIG BOYS' Harley,

　　　　　The little bit on the side you thought
　　　　　Never ever could
　　　　　In a month of Sundays
　　　　　Possibly come good…

WILKIE: But now it seems us 'also-rans'
　　　　Are suddenly front-runners;
　　　　To the major parties we're even seen
　　　　Potentially as 'stunners'.

KATTER: We've only to flutter an eyelash
In their general direction
And they all begin to see themselves
With a promising *election!*

WINDSOR: I'm Tony Windsor from New England…
This lovely upland seat I hold
Is a jewel in the Conservative crown,
24-carat gold!

While the Labour vote's at 8 per cent,
Irrigation and water-supply
Are the very humdrum things on which
My voters all rely.

OAKESHOTT: Rob Oakeshott is my name, you'll note
[gabbling] I'm a much *younger* man…
Lyne's my electorate and I have
This altogether you-beaut plan

To work for government unity,
And my personal position
Is to do away with conflict and
All the costs of long-division;

Let's all join hands in parliament,
Do away with shaking fists!
I know, I know, they're calling me
The last of idealists.

But that's how it is, with me, friends,
And that's how it will stay.
I get the grey vote up here, too,
I'm like their son, they say!

[KATTER interrupts OAKESHOTT here.]

KATTER: Katter's the name I go by,
But most folks call me 'Bob'.
My dad, when he lived up here,
He had this same big job.

Yep, I'm a maverick from the North
And what is even scarier
My electorate stretches right across
From the Gulf of Carpentaria,

Right through to those big cane fields
On the Pacific Coast…
Look, I'm not one to strut about,
Wear my cowboy hat and boast,

But I'm the farmers' true-blue friend
And you pale-faced southern crowd
Better get it straight so I'll say it, mate,
And say it EXTRA LOUD:

I'm here to put the hobbles on
Your city-slicker Labor,
And remind you half-blind city folk
That your farmer's your best neighbour,

So whoever wins this time around
Had better bloody well heed it:
Our vote counts double or triple now
And you're bloody well gonna need it!

WILKIE: My name is Andrew Wilkie
And my seat is in Tasmania:
– You've heard those other Indies
And I hope my views aren't zanier…

I've got a list of wishes and
Not all of them are new
– Some are for *local* consumption
While some are *national* too.

There's the pulp-mill you'll have heard about:
– I'd like that scuppered pronto,
Or built in some more *needy* place
Like Canberra – or Toronto!

I want a limit placed on pokie bets
And a hospital replacement,
And our Hobart port facility
Moved upstairs from the basement.

Climate change is another thing
That urgently needs upgrading,
And withdrawing our troops from Afghanistan
Now our hopes of winning are fading…

And I almost forgot to mention, there's
Whistle-blower legislation
(A wish-list *does* extend a bit
When you're wishing for the *nation!*).

And – just before you drive off in
Your streamlined horseless carriages,
There's dental care and mental care
As well as same-sex marriages!

I know that on my list are things
That put me close to those
Now snuggling up to Julia,
So you may well suppose

> That when the final tally
> Of *this* shearing-shed is full
> You'll find me there – in *government*
> My ears all stuffed with wool.

TOGETHER: Well, *you* might call us WINDIES
> With the wind now in our sails,
> But *we're* not the ones who're voting for
> Land rights for hermaphrodite whales!

[Exit INDIES]

OZZIE: Now, there's danger for those Coalition MPs who still care
> To speak their piece in Parliament whenever they get there.
> I remember Bill Hayden sayin' once (and he said it with a grin)
> In times like this, he reckoned, even a drover's dog could win!

[Enter COALITION SENATOR who begins to sing to the tune of 'The Old Bullock Dray'.]

COALITION SENATOR: Once the Senate used to be
> A comfy place for us,
> But the latest Senate line-up
> Is a *minus*, not a *plus!*
>
> Since the last election, here
> More Greens than ever lurk:
> – Just waiting there to pounce on us
> And bugger up our good work!
>
> Those who said it wasn't easy
> To be *green* just haven't tried
> Surviving in the Senate, where
> Green dingos love to hide!
>
> Oh, I'd rather be a wallaby
> Or a little potoroo
> Than a Coalition Senator knowing
> What those Greens can do!

[Exit COALITION SENATOR]

OZZIE: While the southern states all voted for
The ALP, a state of war
Existed in the north and west
Where the mining industries faced a test
Of wills and what Canberra said
About a mining tax made *them* see RED.

[Enter two MINERS. They march in truculently with red flags. The song they sing has echoes of James Connell's socialist anthem, The Red Flag. *Background sounds of shovel and pick-axe at work.]*

MINER 1: We mining states are seeing red,
We're fighting for our daily bread!
You southerners, with eyes wide-shut,
We've got big boots to kick your butt!

MINERS: So raise the miners' rights on high!
Tax us too much: it's *you* will die,
And just to make this fact quite clear
To defend ourselves we'll persevere…

MINER 2: By rail and boat we ship our ore
Which other nations pay us for…
You folks down south at times forget:
Without us you'd be deep in debt.

MINERS: So take those blinkers from your eyes:
Without us there's no paradise!
And if you tax us to the 'max'
You'll lose those flash shirts off your backs!

[Exit MINERS.]

Act Four

NEWS MEDIA ANNOUNCER: The Electoral Commission has now announced that official counting in the remaining seats has now been completed.

[OZZIE enters, sings, roughly. to the tune of 'Now that the Ball is Over', waving to the song's rhythm ironically with his arms.]

OZZIE: Now that the counting's over
And all the re-counts too,
Some will be pigs in clover,
Some will be deep in poo.

Some will be treadin' carefully
If their margins are egg-shell thin,
Some will be movin' prayerfully
… Some will be sunk in sin…

Some who were safely seated
With a margin of ten-percent,
Now that they've been defeated
Must wonder where the good times *went*.

Many a hopeful member
Who gave up a well-paid job
Must look to old friends to remember
He was good with a top-spin lob!

Pollies, too, aren't immortal,
Though some seem to think they are,
So that's why some of us chortle
When they suffer their last hurrah.

> In many a child-care centre
> Now toddlers can rest secure,
> No pollies are likely to enter
> When an election is not their lure,
>
> Now hard-hats on work-sites are only
> Worn by the blokes who *work*,
> And classroom kids will feel lonely
> With no pollies to help them shirk.

[OZZIE stands up, stretches, plumps up cushion, sits down again.]

> But Julia then found she'd got herself
> A special problem of her own:
> Quite apart from the Indies, there had been
> A growth in the body politic
> (Not unlike a kidney-stone):
> An uncomfortable situation known as Green.

[OZZIE's wife calls shrilly offstage. OZZIE exits hurriedly. JULIA enters, speaking on her mobile phone.]

JULIA: I'm feeling a little GREEN about the gills
Dr Brown, it might be just a phase
– Something I have to go through, like those ills
At every season's turn, a kind of haze

Blurring my old sense of who I am…
I know it may be just a passing thing
I'll laugh about tomorrow, do be a lamb,
And fit me in today…I know it's Spring,

But recently while I was walking on the range
The old familiar certainties just weren't there…
It could be all that talk of climate change
Or something more pernicious in the air.

> Whatever it is, I only know that I'm
> In need of help. *Please*, could you find the time?

[To the audience. Background music of 'Limbo Rock' with next part of JULIA's speech.]

> I'm not a religious person (as you know),
> And labour in the obstetric sense is not for me,
> But there's a place some people call Limbo
> And that is where I fear, *politically*,
> Our party's stuck until we've fully paid
> Penance for our errors, great and small,
> So we're labouring here in Limbo till we've made
> Amends for important principles we've let fall.

[JULIA exits.]

Act Five

[JULIA enters, smiling.]

JULIA: Well, fortune favours the brave, a poet once said,
And those words must have been echoing in my head!
When I met Dr Brown I found he, too,
Shared my concern for my health and began to woo
Me back to a more *healthy* state of mind
(Some people just can't help themselves being kind…).

[Enter DR BROWN with stethoscope.]

DR BROWN: That greenish tinge you have is bound to pass,
Don't look too often in your looking-glass;
You'll find your future Senate legislation notions
Will now become quite regular parliamentary motions.
But, since it's Wattle Day, let's celebrate…
Why not wear your pearls again, and you'll look great?!.

[Exit JULIA and DR BROWN]

[Enter INDIES]

OAKESHOTT: For seventeen long *exhausting* days
We Indies met together
To see if we couldn't decide which mob
Deserves the better weather.

WINDSOR: Then we discovered Andrew Wilkie
Had already declared *his* hand.
He chose Labor and hoped his voters
Would, most of them, understand.

WILKIE: And then Bob Katter decided
To put on *his* hat and walk.
He chose the bush and the party
That'd give him a chance to talk.

Which left Rob Oakshott here, and me
So we chose to go with Labor
Though our voters may accuse us
Of playing 'beggar your neighbour'.

OAKESHOTT: But Julia and Swannie were happy as Larry
Now Labor had crept back in,
And we all looked forward to helping this new
Golden Age begin!

[JULIA enters, draws back curtains. Throughout JULIA's speech, 'Walking on Sunshine' song is played off-stage.]

JULIA: By drawing back these curtains
We've let the sunshine in!
Rob Oakeshott's disinfectant can
Its healing work begin…

He may be a little long-winded, but
When you've been out in the cold so long,
We can hardly blaming him for chuckling
And singing his sunshine song!

Thank goodness our Education
Revolution that went wrong
Isn't seen as maladministration,
And that horrible kind of 'pong'

From *that* unchecked disaster
Has never ever been spelt
Out as a stinking stuff-up
That everyone should have smelt!

Each time we've learnt a lesson
From the latest gross mistake,
We head off in a fresh direction
Another boo-boo to make!

But, look ahead, you Labor members!
Bid farewell to past sorrow
— If you happen to consider today was good,
Well, wait till you see tomorrow!

Of course there are always cynics,
Who claim to have done their sums,
Who say tomorrow always looks better
— Until tomorrow comes.

[JULIA smiles and exits. Sunshine song fades out. Enter OZZIE.]

OZZIE: Well, if home *is* where the heart is,
Then, Julia's heart was *here*,
Puzzlin' how to shape up
For the rest of her first year!

[Exit OZZIE. Enter JULIA with mobile phone. Madrigal music off-stage.]

JULIA: Hello? Is that the university?
It is? Then I'd like to speak
To a certain Professor Dudley:
I believe he's there this week…

[Brief pause.]

Professor, I'm Julia Gillard
The PM, yes, that's right…
I'm hoping we can arrange to meet
At a later time tonight…

[Lights down.]

Act Six

[Lights up on JULIA on stage, as PROFESSOR DUDLEY enters.]

> Good evening, Professor Dudley,
> Your prompt response is so
> Encouraging… I'm sure you are
> Quite curious to know
>
> Why I have called upon you,
> As it were 'out of the blue'
> But there is an important service
> For *me* that *you* can do.

[DUDLEY nods.]

> I have this little matter which
> I'd like to keep discreet,
> And since Elizabethan Studies is your field,
> Your knowledge may well meet
>
> A special image-need I've got
> For those tricky days ahead:
> If you were Queen Bess and I asked your help
> What would *you* have said?

[DUDLEY ponders briefly. JULIA reacts in various ways to DUDLEY's suggestions.]

DUDLEY: First, no more executions,
> Queen Bess would surely say:
> Choose your cabinet carefully
> And you will win the day.

Dress for success, with colour sense,
No jackets jutting out
– Twenty cameras will be watching you,
Fashionistas ready to shout!

Stay unmarried, if you can:
Your husband is the *realm*,
Your ultimate master is this *state*
No *man* should overwhelm…

Remember to keep the common touch
Each voter understands:
To cure or alleviate many an ill
By the laying-on of hands.

Your image thus would be enhanced
And further glorified
Like that *Women's Weekly* feature which
Brought many to your side.

Unite now, by diversity,
Both Greens and Indies too,
Between religious Right and sceptic Left
As Bessie sought to do.

Don't name your own successor,
However much you're pressed,
For plots will fester, tongues will wag,
And you'll find little rest.

Nor should you encourage favourites
Among your staff at court,
Who knows by what more devious means
Disloyalty can be bought?!

        And while as leader you mightn't claim
        Your place by *divine* election,
        Believe, like Bess, that the work you do
        Is *still* your best protection.

        Move forward, then, like Bess who said,
        'The past cannot be cured.'
        And with these as your ten commandments
        Your place in history's assured.

[JULIA rises.]

JULIA: My deepest thanks to you, kind sir!
            Who knows but, bye and bye,
            When I too walk abroad, the crowds
            May 'Gloriana!' cry…

[Exit JULIA and PROFESSOR DUDLEY.]

NEWS MEDIA ANNOUNCER on TV: As parliament is about to resume, Julia appoints her new ministry. The most notable changes are Peter Garrett to a reduced Education role and Kevin Rudd as the new Minister of Foreign Affairs.

[JULIA is in her office.]

JULIA: The time has come when many a bum
            Is hoping for a seat…
            I've only time for the two that were
            Last mentioned in defeat.

            First, let's have Peter in: that lad
            Having burned the Midnight Oil
            Assures me that he's gone and had
            Enough of shameful toil

> In no-man's-land and learned by heart
> Our simple playground rules
> To justify his new position of:
> Inspector-General of Schools!

[JULIA presses button. PETER GARRETT enters. Background music: 'Midnight Oil' singing 'Beds are burning'.]

JULIA: Come in, come in, but do please leave
Your *guitar* at the door...
Unless you want to strum along
As you've often done before...

> Now, Education as a whole
> We thought too much for you...
> But *here*, take Schools, we think that's as much
> As you could possibly *do*.

[PETER exits.]

JULIA: Well, he took that with a noble grin!
Now, let's have Master Kevin in...

[KEVIN enters.]

JULIA: Hello, Kevin, it's nice to see
Your happy face again,
After those stormy periods
Where we *all* felt the pain...

> But, let's forget those regions drear,
> *[shudders]* Those bitter winds that chilled,
> That storm and tempest's acrimony
> With which some hearts were filled:

> You're back now! With no further fear
> Of retribution (though
> Some ministers aren't thrilled to see you
> With any portfolio).

[KEVIN starts, looks around nervously.]

> Peace, peace, perturbéd spirit!
> Your safest place will be
> (Given your skill at making friends)
> … The Foreign Affairs Ministry!

[JULIA hands KEVIN his portfolio. KEVIN responds with smug gesture.]

JULIA: I know at times of crisis
How deeply one can feel…
I only hope that you may find
Your new post has appeal.

Indeed, I sincerely trust that you
May decide to find it best
To visit…OUTER MONGOLIA
As an excellent brush-up test

Of those linguistic skills of yours
Which *did* take second place
To certain forms of mischief…
But, please, let's not embrace

Such memories which would spoil this chance
To start our lives again
– In politics, too, sweet friendship
May follow times of pain!

Now, I know that at a time like this
It's difficult to say much,
So look: while you're out there in Where-ever-it-is,
Keep well! And…keep in touch!

[KEVIN exits. JULIA's managerial mood collapses.]

JULIA: Show me the way to go home
I'm tired and I want to go to bed,
But those Greens and Indies everywhere
Are twittering in my head…

They're all for euthanasia,
And abortion on demand,
And policies like gay marriages
Lots of voters still can't stand…

Our foreign policy alliance
With the US they want scrapped
And with this and other issues
I'm anything but rapt!

Still in our digital universe
The quicker-than quick 'fix' is 'in',
And whenever we make a new mistake
We can cover it up with 'spin'…

But the cost of living's rising,
And we've lost the battlers' vote,
And whenever the next election comes
We're likely to miss the boat.

[JULIA stands still on stage, facing audience, open hands extended in pleading gesture. Lights down.]

Act Seven

[Late night. Lights up. Julia enters left, looks out through curtains. She is now, as her speech indicates, a resident in the Lodge. Turns back to face audience.]

JULIA: However big the colander,
However fine the sieve,
I cannot (for the life of me)
Forget, or yet forgive.

Some of the folk who visit me
[gestures] Since I moved here to the Lodge
Are only ghosts, but ghosts can be
Very difficult to dodge.

[Ghost of DR BROWN enters, at her left hand]

Good Dr Brown, whose visitings
(As one might well expect)
As my special health professional
I treat with great respect.

[JULIA indicates DR BROWN, now seated at table, writing out prescriptions, pausing, looking up, continuing to write.]

Without his providential care
This place would not be mine,
In the Opposition benches, I,
A lesser light, would shine.

[JULIA advances to front centre stage.]

Who knows but, where I'm standing now,
Bespectacled and smiling,
The ghost of Kevin 07 might well
The media be beguiling…

[Ghost of KEVIN enters right.]

> But yet, though assurances still flow
> From time to time about
> These echoing rooms, I'm still afraid
> I've inherited some doubt.
>
> From those before me, noble ghosts
> Like Gough and Bob, who came
> And went (alas, before their time)
> Whose monumental flame
>
> Flickered at the will of those
> Who longed to take *their* place,
> And were cast into outer darkness
> Where often at night I face
>
> This prospect too...And so it is
> That frequently I turn
> And step into this mirror where
> Both past and future burn...

[Lights down on JULIA, up on mirror-self which now confronts her other self.]

MIRROR-JULIA: The carbon tax... Now that's *one* thing
> That *almost* I regret:
> If only before that election
> I'd just been *vague*...and yet
>
> To change a No to a Yes is surely
> What *men* do all the time
> – So why on earth, for a *woman* PM,
> Is it such a mortal crime?!

Circumstances alter cases,
– From here it's plain to see
That a carbon tax *is* what we need
(Ask Kevin – he'd agree…),

But Kevin was Copenhagen-bound
And probably still thought
Hamlet was set in the capital
And not in a Danish port.

[JULIA gestures off stage.]

Asylum seekers – they're another
Problem I must face:
Why must the Middle East remain
A politically *murderous* place?

[Four ILLEGAL IMMIGRANTS protesters circle JULIA throughout this next speech, each carrying a placard: EAST TIMOR, MANUS ISLAND, MALAYSIA, and (marching on his/her own: NAURU).]

East Timor seemed at first the shot
– But it turned out that I had
Assumed I'd got their 'OK' when it seemed
I hadn't…that was *bad*.

Then Manus Island next I tried,
But that, too, hit the deck.
Malaysia, then? The signs were good,
But it ended up a wreck.

If now I've opted for Nauru
(Plus motels and whatever)
With more and more boats coming in
It doesn't seem very clever.

[JULIA now steps out of mirror-frame and pauses. Phone rings. JULIA answers, listens briefly, then hangs up. Faces audience, makes wry face, hands spread in dismay.]

> Good Dr Brown, I'm told, is gone,
> But I guess I'll have to soldier on…
> As my physician he was rather nice;
> Who *now* can I turn to for advice?

[JULIA gestures around.]

> This Lodge that I'm now living in
> Is only mine so long
> As I dance to someone else's tune
> And also sing their song.
>
> Each week I stand on a slippery slope
> ('Ms Sisyphus' you might call me),
> I wake at night and ask myself
> What new shocks can befall me?
>
> How green, once, did my valley seem,
> In those years at Slater & Gordon!
> But around me now my *enemies*
> Are drawing in their cordon….
>
> As a lawyer I early learnt
> What very householder knows:
> That mortgages can be ruinous,
> Should ever the bank foreclose…
>
> I'm mortgaged to the hilt right now,
> And feel my isolation
> – How can I balance out my debts
> And the *nation's* expectations?

It's a battle all the way
And at times I know it shows,
They say my time is running out,
I've copped a lot of blows,

That's why I wave my hands around
And my eyes at times declare,
Like a traumatised soldier, I've acquired
That *thousand-yards stare*...

[JULIA advances to front of stage for her final reflections.]

I'm judged for lacking judgement which *they* say
Goes with the territory; they forget
I'm far from free in any case; my way
Is booby-trapped with options I'll regret.

As PM, until Kevin's polls went bad,
Kevin had *power* to back up his *position*
– That's a luxury, you see, I've never had:
I took the *crown*, but lacked that key condition.

The choices that I've made at times may seem
Free choices, but they *aren't*; I'm hemmed about
By those who have a very different dream
Of government, even so without
Their backing, well, I'm dead…It's after all
A numbers game (I count them through
Each day now. It's *all* that I can do.).

[Lights down slowly on JULIA standing stiffly erect, facing the audience. JULIA exits. OZZIE enters, remains standing. Noise of kids yelling off-stage. OZZIE points off-stage, indicating them. Sits down in lounge chair.]

OZZIE: You hear that racket out there?
It's those game-shows kids now play
– Those grandkids of mine are all the same,
All peas in an iPod day!

Here's me tryin' to make some sense
Of *my* weird generation,
The one supposed to have sufficient
Clues to run this nation.
And Labor's *still* in limbo;
Seems we've been there quite a spell:
Halfway to Heaven
And at least halfway to Hell.

Yeah, the longer I sit here wonderin'
What on earth we're headin' for
– The more I reckon I'd better keep
One eye on an EXIT door!

[OZZIE screws around in lounge chair to face left stage exit-door. Then turns back to face audience, with philosophic shrug. Fade out.]

Act Eight

[Lights up. OZZIE still facing audience, but now with startled expression.]

OZZIE: Well blow me down with a feather, if
The very next thing you know:
Kevin Rudd's back here in Oz
To have another go!

He's lookin' for the Party vote to kick
Our lady PM out
– I'll betcha he'll come on pretty strong,
Without a doubt!

[Light down on OZZIE, up on KEVIN confidently entering. KEVIN addresses audience as if a Party meeting.]

KEVIN: Those dark clouds which the PM thought
Were just a passing thing
Were merely an ironic omen of
My second Spring!
You can have me back right now
As your *leader*, my dear people!
And the sun will brightly shine again
On our Party's steeple…

And I, having harrowed Hell, will then
Rise and return
So that hope and faith may both once more
In my dear people burn.

As you may see, I wear my wounds
With a very special pride
– Let that miserable interregnum
Now be cast aside.

[Adds steely tone.]

> But any of those faithless ones
> Who once had willed my death,
> I'll haunt those villains as Banquo
> Haunted *vile* Macbeth…
>
> Let Kevin 07 be again your king
> And he'll walk beaming forth,
> Behold, to loud hosannas,
> South, East, and especially *North*.

[KEVIN stands, beaming, arms still raised as lights go down on him and up on OZZIE.]

OZZIE: Yeah, well it just wasn't to be:
When the Party's vote was in
Kevin found himself dumped again
In the same old wheelie-bin.

> My Dad used to often say
> 'If you want a bit of advice:
> A decent cook doesn't ever need
> To boil his cabbages twice.'

[Suddenly in serious tone.]

> And – I was about to give the game away
> And watch some other show,
> When Julia herself just copped
> A very bitter blow.

[Fade out OZZIE. Lights up on JULIA, entering slowly left, dressed in black].

JULIA: Sometimes a personal grief will be the spur
To build up animus in him (or *her*).
And when your political enemy puts a name
To all your pent-up feelings, then a flame
Sets every sense alight! A fire

[Becomes animated.]

Leaps through the branches, a great sense of loss
Is lit by anger's lightning…so it was
My personal passion worked so well because
When Tony Abbott touched the tinder-box
Which was my grieving heart, the shocks
Went all around the world
Purple flags of anger everywhere unfurled!

[Exit JULIA affirmatively. Enter DANCING GIRLS, singing.]

DANCING GIRLS: Misogyny, misogyny!
That word has many progeny:
Dear Julia could never have guessed
How north and south and east and west
Even the most down-hearted fem
Found a new word to strike at *them!*
As lightning starts a forest fire
So this word summed up *all* our ire;
The earth was scorched, in every ear
Misogyny ruled the femisphere!

Misogyny, misogyny!
It's only a word in the dictionary
But it has more power on a woman's lips
Than a whole chorus-line of hips!
There's no pussyfooting around
With a word like that; then every sound
Is meant to make many a girlfriend quiver

And push her boyfriend into the river!
– Some words mean just what you want them to be
And that's the magic of misogyny!

[Exit DANCING GIRLS. Sombre music begins low offstage. TONY enters disconsolately. Looks up and addresses audience, shrugging.]

TONY: Well what's a man to do?
With all this hullabloo
I am a *man* when all is said and done
– And being a rock-chopper too
Isn't worth a brass razoo
When Emily's List has got you on the run.

Okay, I'm a *blokey* bloke,
But now it's no longer a joke:
Budgie-smugglers and a hairy chest can both of them be
A way to put you down.
Make out you're a bloody clown
Even if you *have* got an economics degree…

[Shrugs again.]

Ah well… That's how it goes:
There are pats on the head and then blows;
Whatever the game is, they're just waiting for you;
If you're aiming to be a saint
Then party politics ain't
The sort of occupation you oughta pursue…

[Exit, downhearted, shrugging… Spotlight up on OZZIE. He starts thumping in disgust a newspaper he's been reading.]

OZZIE: Dunno about these paper polls
– There's bugger-all way of knowin'
With all these 'Undecided' souls
Which way the winds are blowin'.

Who wants to back a loser?
When you front up to the bar
And you're the only one in the boozer
To be called a prize galah?

[Light down on OZZIE. Enter JULIA in lycra tights and top. Light also now on pole-dance pole. JULIA face audience, gestures towards pole.]

JULIA: Usually, you know, I never
Comment on polls

[Strokes pole thoughtfully.]

Except of course when me and mine
Look set to kick some goals…
I'm a Windy City football fan,
The 'Bulldog Breed', that's me
[gestures] And with my extra special specs
I can see what I can see…
Some polls can give us lots of hope
Instead of the same old blather;
They help you choose the kind of soap
You can work up into a lather.

[Stands by pole, looks up at it briefly, then turns back to face audience again.]

Poll-dancing's just the game to keep
Those media folk quite busy
– You think I'm really going to climb
This pole here? I'd get *dizzy*…

My lycra costume's just to fool
Those easily fooled, remember?
So here I'll stay, come what come may.
– At least until September!

Yes, now that I've set an election date
It's given me lots of room
– Some say I've left it far too late
And prophesy my doom,

But when I took that cardboard crown
I knew I was on my own;
Nobody needed to tell me that
It's lonely on a throne...

If now I could only re-create
That incendiary gender fire
My prospects in September
Would be infinitely higher!

[Exit JULIA, smiling wryly, but exits with a positive step. MAN and WOMAN enter from right and left stage. They smile to each other, then turn and face audience.]

MAN: They say there's going to be a showdown
But nobody knows just when...

WOMAN: It's a showdown that's a slowdown,
That's been on and off again.

MAN: The whole town's keeping indoors;
No one wants to cop some lead

WOMAN: Because all we know for sure is:
You can end up very dead.

MAN: The union blokes in the old saloon
Are drinking their whisky straight.
They're trembling in their singlets
And betting each-way on their fate.

WOMAN: Like a western movie I saw once
(*High Noon*, with Gary Cooper).
That lovely girl Grace Kelly was in it;
She was a Quaker and looked 'super'.

MAN: Yes, I saw that movie, too;
But it was easy then to tell:
Gary Cooper was the hero
And the bad guys were from hell.

WOMAN: Well, any moment now we'll see
Our Terrible Two stride out
To face each other at last and put
The issue beyond all doubt.

        This showdown's been the talk of town
For what seems years and years;
We all knew it was coming
And got ready with our tears…

[MAN begins looking at his watch.]

MAN: The hour is getting late and still
This 'talk-and-stalk' goes on
By the time they get to shoot it out
Our interest will be gone!

        A dreary Boot Hill future waits
For either Quick-Gun Kevin,
Or Ms Julia's going to find herself
On a one-way trip to Heaven.

[WOMAN now falls to her knees with prayerful hands, pleading to audience.]

WOMAN: Oh please, won't someone beg them, *please*,
To put a stop to all this fuss,
Or the ultimate shoot-out victims
Surely will be – US!

[Slow fade-out with WOMAN on her knees still, facing audience, being now comforted by MAN.]

Act Nine

[Enter KEVIN. He's reading Shakespeare's Richard III. Waggles book, sits and starts to read from tagged place. Looks up at audience, following brief reading. Speaks in blank verse.]

KEVIN: Funny how they've recently found
              The bones of Richard III, that sad king whom
              Tudors and Elizabethans slew to prove
              History is always written by the victors...
              Bill Shakespeare was too smart to risk
              His neck for a Plantagenet. Now I wonder
              Will history in *our* Party's name be written
              By me or my supplanter, that assassin?
              Or by some plotter hovering in the wings,
              Scheming their way into that paper crown,
              Shaping acceptance speeches, packed with necessary
              Humility and high purpose; could *their* reign
              Be a 'clean start' when in one kitchen or another
              All the knives are blunt or somehow stained?

[KEVIN shrugs, walks up and down, faces audience again and gestures with hands.]

              Who knows? *I* don't, but like the sphinx,
              Crouch with lion's paws, content to wait;
              Patience points the way for my return:
              I know that patience in the past
              Hasn't been my cardinal virtue, but
              I still have forgotten nothing, and forgiven less...
              Daily I polish up my armoury
              And mark the days off on my calendar
              – The Ides of September haven't gone, while she
              Must walk in the Forum many a breathless day.
              Already both caucus and the back-bench tremble
              While I stand ready in the interim.

[KEVIN stops suddenly, consults his watch.]

> Oh dear…I feel a photo-op coming on.
> If you'll excuse me now, I must be gone.

[Exit KEVIN, with a gracious bow to the audience].

[OZZIE enters with newspaper, looks at front page, thumps paper disgustedly, shakes head, addresses audience.]

OZZIE: I was drivin' along the other day,
My thoughts elsewhere (the usual way),
The missus was checkin' the shoppin' list
(There's always somethin' we might've missed),

When, out of the blue, this old Barina
Sneaked up on the outside (I should've seen 'er)
And damned near rammed us, the way they can
When they don't show up on either hand
In that one space that's everyone's curse,
The one that's not covered by your reverse
Mirror or the side-one either…It could've been worse
Of course – and then I'd reckon
Disaster in *one* of its forms would beckon…
So, after that silly bugger had passed,
And I'd given him a bit of a blast,
And I'd stopped thumpin' the steerin'-wheel
(As you do., expressin' the way you feel),
I suddenly thought of how this kind
Of thing that catches you from behind,
Is somethin' that happens a lot of the time
To all of us whether committin's some crime
Or goin' about our daily biz
– It's somethin' about the way things is…
It's a traffic hazard; but, like it or not,
Everybody's got this one blind spot.

[OZZIE pauses, to let this sink in.]

> You're drivin' along on this road called Life,
> With a bird, or a pal, or your own good wife
> When, all of sudden, like that Barina with me,
> You're a mudguard away from calamity!
> I mean, you take our PM now:
> She's often got me scratchin' my brow
> Over some things she comes out with, such
> As the recent time when, to keep in touch
> She told everyone from now on they'd see
> The *Real Julia*…well, bugger me,
> Just how many Julias has she got?!
> By the sound of it there's quite a lot;
> It's like in that TV game-show where
> All the contestants have to swear
> That they're the real Englebert Humperdink
> And you've got to have a really good think
> And try to pick out the genuine one…
> Now, on a game-show it can be fun,
> But when it's your country's leader, you worry;
> What if she got dressed one day in a hurry
> And put on the *Bodgie Julia* dress
> Well – the whole of Australia could end in a mess!

[OZZIE thumps newspaper.]

> So, when I see somebody like that (ahem!)
> Radio host with our own PM
> Playin' the Easter Bunny, I know
> Another blind spot is beginnin' to show…
> When I hear that she's crooked on ties that are blue
> Or see pictures of her knittin' a little woolly roo
> I'm amazed that she's managin' that same brave smile
> That's kept her goin' for mile after mile
> With her mirror fogged up, both side and reverse,
> Given that the traffic's only gonna get worse.

But it's no wonder our pollies look fagged,
When they know they've zigged instead of zagged,
And there's journos on hand with all of their quaint
Questions, like 'How come you've scraped off some paint?'

[OZZIE folds newspaper, prepares to get up.]

Seems the bigger that parliament gets, the fewer
The ones who're shovellin' up the manure;
You vote for some joker and the last time they're seen
They're way outa sight in that big machine!

Yep, everyone's got blind spots, lots of batsmen who
Were facin' up to old Shane Warne certainly had 'em, too.
All of us have got 'em, not just Aussie 'pollies',
– But still we'll find we're likely to pay a big price for *their* follies!

[OZZIE stands up, shakes his head sadly. Exits.]

Act Ten

[JULIA and KEVIN enter from left and right stage. Each gives the other a wintry smile and then face audience.]

JULIA: After all the votes were in
On that dark winter day,
And the casualties were in the bin
And the New Order under way,

What could we two say to each other,
After all the cross words said,
With so many fantasised dreams to smother
On the pot-holed street ahead?

KEVIN: Well, why am I expected to forgive
The butcher who held the knife,
Who denied me the chance I was given to live
And learn from the facts of life?

JULIA: Excuse me, this wasn't just me, alone
Brought this whole business about,
For behind me, as behind every throne,
Were faction-leaders with clout,
Who saw their own future also at stake
In what we as leaders decide
– Is it any wonder we also make
Tail-gating part of the ride?

No, I don't imagine that either of us ever
Will forgive one another for what
Each will continue to see forever
Only the *other's* blind spot…

[Exit KEVIN. JULIA pauses, approaches front stage, speaks reflectively.]

JULIA: If I could bring together in my mind
Those three things that mean so much to me:
What *was*, what *is*, and what is *yet to be,*
I think that I would find
The answer to so much that troubles me
In this lonely world where, once again,
Being a woman in a world of men,
Where I stand now I'm anything but free…

As a student activist, I knew success,
As a lawyer later too I fought for fair,
In parliament as well I did my share,
(My No meant No, my Yes meant usually Yes...)

Now, as PM, if I could once more find
A *personal* way to integrate these three:
What *was*, what *is*, and *what is yet to be*
I would feel much easier in my mind.

I've been in Limbo at the Lodge. Before I came here,
I was made an offer I could not refuse
When it was put to me, I just thought 'Why not?
– It's there for the taking, what have you got to lose?'

I've never had the luxury some others have had
(There was always Caesar's shadow at *my* door...).
Too many let the past define the future,
But I'll not be any political party's whore!

I'm fully aware of the various party factions,
I know the games they play,
But I'm not a mug to be used and abused
And then, when it suits them, thrown away.

> I've been at the top for three years now
> And yet it feels like I've just begun.
> Wherever I look there are hills to climb
> And hardly a glimpse of the sun.

[TONY now joins KEVIN and JULIA. They confront each other tensely forming a triangle. MAN and WOMAN appear again. They stand; one to the right and one to the left of the political triangle. As MAN begins to chant the Blame Game song, the three political combatants begin to slowly circle each other, pointing a condemnatory index finger at the one in front.]

MAN: We do it best in parliament, especially if you
Are part of the present government; here's what you can do:
If anything you fancy doesn't seem to turn out right
Then here's the best solution (you can use it day and night)
– If you're running up a deficit where a surplus was before,
It's the other party's error (there are always plenty more),
Like a baby that's abandoned at some orphanage's door
You can blame it on those persons whose behaviour you deplore.

MAN and WOMAN Together:
It's the blame-game,
It'll cover every sin,
It's the blame-game
You can nearly always win.

It's the blame-game,
It's the *other* mob, you know,
It's the blame-game,
And it started long ago…

WOMAN: When Adam was a little lad, he learned to play the game,
And when Eve appeared his alibi was practically the same;
He said Eve was the really guilty one; she ate the apple *first*
And since *her* sin preceded his, it obviously was the worst.
It's the blame-game, it started way back then

– God wasn't fooled, and ever since, both women and, yes, men
Have always tried to steal the biggest fig leaf from each other
For each has got, for their mortal lot, a lot of sins to cover.
So if at times it seems as though you've heard this game before
Then you've simply been aware of a universal law…
There was once a Queensland pollie who was wise enough to know
That admitting every error enabled him to go
And *humbly*, unlike Adam, apologise, and then
Tomorrow, or soon after, he'd do the same again.
The moral of this lesson, the moral of this song
Is, if there is no-one else to blame whenever you've got it wrong
You should practise at a mirror until you look your honest best
But until you can convince yourself…you should let the matter rest.

[At the final verse JULIA, KEVIN and TONY slow to a halt, each still pointing to the one in front. They freeze as a tableau as the last verse ends. Lights down. A funeral bell begins tolling, to signify the crucial vote of the ALP caucus.]

RADIO ANNOUNCER: Another caucus vote has been called by the ALP to decide the leadership of the Federal Party.

[Then a drum beats softly but insistently as a large white screen is pushed on stage to record the two events: the ALP caucus vote, and the critical State of Origin 2 Rugby League clash. Projected on the screen, excited preparations for the State of Origin 2 involving maroon or blue dressed rugby league fans. This is followed by a TV shot of JULIA, smiling, as she walks with party supporters towards ALP caucus meeting, followed by a TV shot of KEVIN walking, confident but alone, towards the same meeting. Drum beats rising quickly to climax as result of caucus vote appears on the screen: Kevin 57, Julia 45. KEVIN enters stage right, smiling easily at audience.]

KEVIN: Those folks who know their scriptures
              In the twelfth chapter of St John
              Will remember a man called Lazarus;
              He was dead, but was *raised* and lived on…

> So, you too now see here before you
> One who was slain, but arose,
> Resurrected as you see, by the Party
> Despite all the villainy of foes.

[Gestures, as if casting off cerements.]

> So, away with the grave-clothes which bound me,
> And the cloth which once covered my face
> – No more will the last three years hound me,
> Behold, they've left hardly a trace!

[KEVIN begins to waltz sedately to background music of 'My Bonny Lies Over the Ocean', arms held high in triumph.]

> Oh, once more I have a great caucus,
> As splendid as any could be,
> If only they will follow my wishes
> I'll lead them to victory!

[Background music continues to rise, as KEVIN, smiling beatifically to audience, waltzes off stage.]

Final Curtain

www.ingramcontent.com/pod-product-compliance
Lightning Source LLC
Chambersburg PA
CBHW071034080526
44587CB00015B/2607